Yoga
DOGS

DAN BORRIS

ABRAMS IMAGE
NEW YORK

Editor: David Cashion
Designer: Kara Strubel
Production Manager: Alison Gervais

Library of Congress Cataloging-in-Publication Data

Borris, Daniel.
  Yoga dogs / Daniel Borris.
       p. cm.
  ISBN 978-0-8109-9682-3 (alk. paper)
  1. Dogs—Pictorial works. 2. Photography of dogs. 3. Dogs—Humor.
I. Title.
  SF430.B67 2011
  636.702'07--dc22
                                    2010036794

Published in 2011 by Abrams Image, an imprint of ABRAMS. All
rights reserved. No portion of this book may be reproduced, stored
in a retrieval system, or transmitted in any form or by any means,
mechanical, electronic, photocopying, or otherwise, without written
permission from the publisher.

Printed and bound in U.S.A.
10 9 8 7 6 5 4

Abrams Image books are available at special discounts when purchased
in quantity for premiums and promotions as well as fundraising or
educational use. Special editions can also be created to specification. For
details, contact specialmarkets@abramsbooks.com or the address below.

115 West 18th Street
New York, NY 10011
www.abramsbooks.com

FOR ALEJANDRA,
whose compassion and love for animals is boundless.

INTRODUCTION

Yoga Dogs is the first fully illustrated guide to yoga created by dogs for dogs (with the assistance of a few humans purely for technical purposes). Yoga for dogs isn't simply a matter of applying two-legged poses to four-legged yogis. The differences are more subtle and fundamental. For example, chakras run in a vertical line up the human spine, but in dogs, that energy field follows a horizontal path— a seemingly simple but important distinction.

Any canine can and should practice yoga. From show dogs and working dogs to mixed breeds and even basic squirrel chasers, we all can enjoy its benefits. Even if you spend a lot of your day lying around the house, only going for the occasional walk, it's important to stretch, stay flexible, and keep in shape.

For the more ambitious among us, it should be noted that many "Best in Show" winners practice yoga. A fairly large percentage of today's top competitors use yoga to keep their bodies supple and their minds focused. As you know, it's not easy remaining calm while someone's running you around in circles in front of an audience. One champion reports, "Yoga has put me back in touch with why I compete. I no longer get caught up in the nerves and expectations. Now during a show, I find myself 'in the zone,' and not even my trainer's frantic behavior affects me." Another says, "I no longer feel judged. I'm more secure with who I am as a dog." Out in the work world, Shepherds speak of a stronger connection—"a feeling of Oneness"—with their flocks and herds. And one mixed-breed practitioner claims yoga has led him to experience a deeper, more unified sense of self: "For a long time,

I used to ask myself, 'Am I a Beagle? Am I a Schnauzer? Am I a Poodle? But through yoga, I realized that I'm just me. A Beagaschnauzapoo." It's also a practice that's beneficial for all ages. One elderly thirteen-year-old Chihuahua living in Miami offered, "Of course, there are the physical benefits, but it's not about only that for me. It's also about being in touch with my inner puppy."

Little is known about the exact origins of Yoga Dogs. The common belief is that Yoga Humans copied the movements of various animals as inspiration for what eventually became yoga poses. They carefully developed and refined these poses over the centuries. To outside appearances, it seems that things came full circle in the past few years when dogs began practicing these human poses, but recent evidence suggests a different history. Photographs have been found tracing Yoga Dogs back more than one hundred years. Several of the earliest images feature dogs practicing yoga in India, and additional photos taken in New York document the arrival of Yoga Dogs to the American shores in the early 20th century. It can probably be assumed that Yoga Dogs existed before the advent of photography, but they kept their practice of the flexible arts quiet to keep humans from, well, freaking out. As we know, it's really only been recently that our homo sapien companions have discovered the full range of our abilities and talents. It's no longer just "sit and stay" or "fetch" for Fido. The (peaceful) Great Terrier Rebellion of the 21st century changed all that . . . but those stories are for another book. The purpose of this volume that you're holding in your paws is meant to inspire all dogs to attain better health and self-realization through the practice of yoga. If you're a beginner, start with the poses you're most comfortable with and go slow. Enjoy the process; yoga is a journey, not a destination. (And to any humans reading this: Enough with the "Downward-Facing Dog" jokes. We get it. And frankly, we invented it.)

An unusual, modern snapshot from 1965
of West Coast Yoga Dog Romeo, taken
on California's Zuma Beach.

This tintype dated 1898 and taken in Bombay (Mumbai) India is one of the earliest-known images of a Yoga Dog master. It is believed that Guru Lilipalko founded the first Yoga Dog school in Bombay.

*In this rare hand-tinted portrait from the Kutte Ka Studio in Agra (c. 1900), we see Swami Chote in Kukkutasana pose. This swami known for his diminutive size (*chote *means* tiny *in Hindi) and amazing flexibility became a sensation throughout India at the turn of the 19th century.*

This early 20th-century photograph is believed to be of Jake, a student at the secret East Meets West Yoga Dog Studio. Located on West 17th Street in Manhattan, this was the first Yoga Dogs school outside of India.

Yogi Rocky Barkjan, the original
Hundalini Yoga Dog master.

*Guru Sunahare Mela, spiritual leader of
the Hundalini Yoga Dog lineage.*

If you meet the Buddha on the road,

sniff him and remember his scent well.

Viparita Salabhasana

INVERTED LOCUST

Strengthens abdomen, lower back, buttocks, and legs
Boosts heart rate
Improves absorption of oxygen
Increases flexibility in spine
Stimulates cardiovascular and digestive systems
Opens energy channels along front of body

Those who are free of resentful thoughts (and fleas)

will surely find peace.

Vrksasana

TREE POSE VARIATION

Stretches inner thighs, chest, and shoulders
Strengthens calves, ankles, and spine
Improves sense of balance

Salamba Sarvangasana

SUPPORTED SHOULDER STAND

Stretches neck and shoulders
Improves digestion
Alleviates insomnia
Reduces fatigue
Relieves stress
Calms the brain

Peace comes from within.

(And from pork chops that fall off the dinner table.)

Ardha Matsyendrasana

HALF LORD OF THE FISHES

Stretches neck, shoulders, and hips
Energizes spine
Reduces asthma
Relieves fatigue and back pain

Eka Hasta Adho Mukha Vrksasana

ONE-ARM HANDSTAND

Stretches shoulders, abdomen, and arms
Improves sense of balance

One does not chase the car

in order to catch the car.

Hansasana
SWAN POSE

Strengthens spine, arms, and wrists
Tones abdomen

Adho Mukha Vrksasana

HANDSTAND

Stretches belly
Strengthens shoulders, arms, and wrists
Improves sense of balance
Relieves stress
Calms the brain

Calmness of mind is reached

by cultivating friendliness toward the happy,

compassion for the unhappy,

delight in the virtuous,

and indifference toward UPS men.

Vrischikasana

SCORPION POSE

Tones spinal nerves
Increases blood flow to the brain and mind-body coordination
Revitalizes body systems

Three things cannot be hidden long:

the sun, the moon, and the truth.

Okay, maybe four if that nosy Schnauzer next door

sees where you've buried your bone.

Adho Mukha Svanasana

DOWNWARD-FACING DOG

Strengthens arms and legs
Stretches shoulders, hamstrings, calves, arches, and hands
Improves digestion
Energizes the body

Virabhadrasana

WARRIOR II

Stretches shoulders, chest, and lungs
Stretches and strengthens legs and ankles
Increases stamina
Relieves back pain

Bhujangasana

COBRA POSE

Tones back
Improves concentration
Relieves and prevents lower back pain

A man is not considered a good man because he is a good talker.

A dog is not considered a good dog because he is a good barker.

Urdhva Mukha Svanasana

UPWARD-FACING DOG

Stretches shoulders, chest, lungs, and abdomen
Firms buttocks
Strengthens spine, arms, and wrists
Improves posture
Stimulates abdominal organs
Reduces asthma

Virabhadrasana I

WARRIOR I

Stretches neck, shoulders, chest, and lungs
Stretches and strengthens thighs, calves, and ankles
Strengthens shoulders, back, and arms

Adho Mukha Vrksasana

HANDSTAND

Stretches belly
Strengthens shoulders, arms, and wrists
Improves sense of balance

Going outside is good.

Coming inside is good.

It's all good.

Utthita-Hasta-Padangusthasana

BIG TOE POSE

Strengthens thighs and calves
Improves digestion
Relieves anxiety and stress
Calms the brain

Ardha-Chandrasana

HALF-MOON POSE

Strengthens spine, abdomen, and ankles
Improves coordination, digestion, and sense of balance

Two paws clap and there is no sound;

what is the sound of one paw?

Vrksasana

TREE POSE VARIATION

Stretches shoulders, chest, and groin
Strengthens spine and ankles
Reduces flat feet
Relieves sciatica

Better than a thousand hollow words

is one word that brings peace.

Especially if that one word is

"Who wants their tummy rubbed?"

Bitilasana

CAT-COW VARIATION

Massages spine and belly organs
Stretches neck and front torso

Halasana

PLOW POSE

Stretches shoulders and spine
Relieves stress
Reduces fatigue

To conquer oneself is a greater feat than conquering others.

Unless it's conquering that whiny ball of Siamese fuzz

behind the fence that never shuts up.

Trikonasana

TRIANGLE POSE

Stretches and strengthens thighs, knees, and ankles
Relieves stress
Reduces anxiety, flat feet, and neck pain

Parivrtta Trikonasana

REVERSE TRIANGLE

Stretches hips and spine
Opens chest
Improves breathing
Relieves mild back pain

Sometimes you're the dog,

sometimes you're the hydrant.

Virasana

HERO POSE

Strengthens arches
Improves digestion and relieves gas
Reduces asthma and high blood pressure

Supta Padangusthasana

RECLINING BIG TOE POSE

Stretches hips, thighs, hamstrings, and calves
Strengthens knees
Improves digestion
Reduces flat feet and high blood pressure

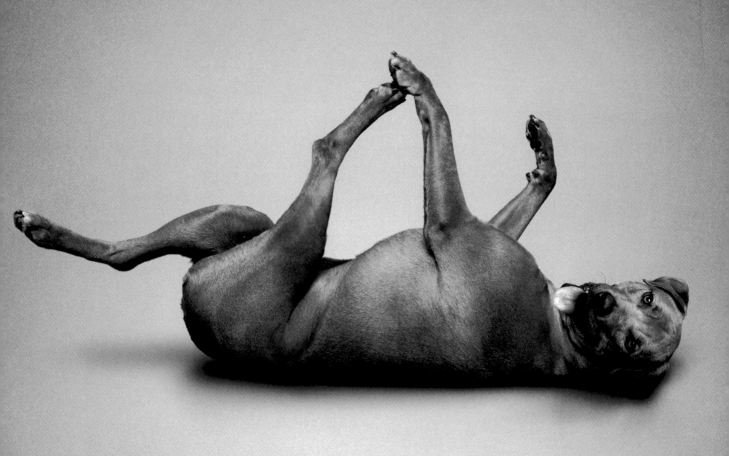

When you realize how perfect everything is,

you will tilt your snout back

and laugh at the sky.

Tittibhasana

FIREFLY POSE

Stretches back torso and inner groin
Strengthens arms and wrists
Tones belly
Improves sense of balance

All that we are is the result of what we have smelt.

What we smell, we become.

Savasana

CORPSE POSE

Relaxes body
Reduces fatigue, headache, high blood pressure, and insomnia

Paripurna Navasana

FULL BOAT POSE

Improves digestion
Stimulates kidneys
Relieves stress

Meditation brings wisdom;

lack of meditation leaves ignorance;

lack of wisdom means you won't figure out

how to open the pantry door where the Scooby Snacks are kept.

So meditate real good.

Padangusthasana

TOE STAND

Strengthens belly
Relieves arthritis in hips and leg joints
Balances and focuses body and mind

Bakasana

CRANE POSE

Stretches upper back, arms, and wrists
Strengthens abdomen

There are only two mistakes one can make along the road to truth:

not going all the way, and not starting.

And pretending you didn't eat that pair of Manolo Blahniks!

Upavistha Konasana

WIDE-ANGLE SEATED FORWARD BEND

Stretches insides and backs of legs
Strengthens spine
Stimulates abdominal organs
Calms the brain

Parsva Bakasana

SIDE CROW POSE

Strengthens arms and wrists
Tones spine and belly
Improves sense of balance

Do not dwell in the past, do not dream of the future;

concentrate the mind on the present moment

and on avoiding mailboxes while riding in the car

with your head out the window.

Virabhadrasana III

WARRIOR III

Strengthens shoulders, back, legs, and ankles
Tones abdomen
Improves sense of balance and posture

Virabhadrasana

WARRIOR II

Stretches shoulders, chest, and lungs
Stretches and strengthens legs and ankles
Increases stamina
Relieves back pain

You yourself,

as much as anybody in the entire universe,

deserve love and affection,

and a warm spot in the bed where someone just got up.

Natarajasana

LORD OF THE DANCE

Stretches shoulders, chest, abdomen, and thighs
Strengthens legs and ankles
Improves sense of balance

Every object, every being, is a jar full of delight.

But a jar full of peanut butter is really something.

Eka Hasta Adho Mukha Vrksasana

ONE-ARM HANDSTAND

Improves sense of balance
Relieves stress
Calms the brain

Garudasana

EAGLE POSE

Stretches thighs, hips, shoulders, and upper back
Improves concentration
Improves sense of balance

Only when my leash is off
can I achieve non-attachment.

Krounchasana

HERON POSE

Stretches hamstrings
Stimulates abdominal organs and heart

Hanumanasana

MONKEY POSE

Stretches shoulders, abdomen, arms, thighs, groin, and hamstrings
Relieves stress

Yoga is not possible for those who eat too much

or those who do not eat at all;

those who sleep too much or who stay awake.

But if you're not in that yoga mood,

better to err on the side of too much.

Baddha Konasana

BOUND ANGLE POSE

Reduces asthma, flat feet, and high blood pressure
Improves general circulation
Stimulates heart
Relieves anxiety, fatigue, and mild depression
Soothes sciatica

Dhyana

SELF-INQUIRY MEDITATION

Builds sense of purpose
Centers self
Quiets mind

ACKNOWLEDGMENTS

Without the partnership of Alejandra Diaz-Berrio (the other half of *Yoga Dogs* and the other half of my marriage), *Yoga Dogs* would not exist. Not only does she work with animals, offer valuable criticism (not always happily received, though almost always right), organize photo shoots, research poses, and do yoga, but she does them all straight from her heart. And for that, there cannot be thanks enough.

Special thanks to Jamie Stolarski for his invaluable collaboration and assistance in making these photographs come to life, and to Rick Valdez for his craft and artistic eye.

Much appreciation goes to the San Antonio Animal Defense League for opening their doors and sharing their beautiful puppies for adoption.

Of course, endless thanks to all the amazing Yoga Dogs and their companions for sharing their time, talent, and willingness to participate.

Thank you to agents Paul Wheeler at Looking Good Licensing and Julie Newman of Jewel Branding for making this book possible.

Alejandra and I would like to thank our families for their trust and support. Thanks especially go to my daughters, Isabelle and Sophie, for their patience while our lives went to the dogs, and for humoring me by laughing at the right things at the right times.

Thank you to editor David Cashion for his many superb contributions.

To Mela and Snoosh, our divine and magical yoga dog and yoga cat, both true wonders of nature, we offer our humble gratitude.

And finally to Joy Nicholson and Otis, the original sparks of *Yoga Dogs*, thank you.

No one saves us but ourselves.

No one can and no one may.

We ourselves must walk the path.

Because the path . . . wait a second . . .

Did someone say WALK?!!!